Wrestling
Greats

SCOTT STEINER

Ross Davies

The Rosen Publishing Group, Inc.
New York

Published in 2002 by The Rosen Publishing Group, Inc.
29 East 21st Street, New York, NY 10010

Library of Congress Cataloging-in-Publication Data

Davies, Ross.
Scott Steiner / by Ross Davies.—1st ed.
p. cm. — (Wrestling greats)
Includes bibliographical references and index.
Summary: Chronicles professional wrestler Scott Steiner's
rise to fame, controversial behavior, and enduring fan appeal.
ISBN 0-8239-3491-8 (lib. bdg.)
1. Steiner, Scott—Juvenile literature. 2. Wrestlers—United
States—Biography—Juvenile literature. [1. Steiner, Scott.
2. Wrestlers.] I. Title. II. Series.
GV1196.S743 D38 2001
796.812'092—dc21

                                                    2001002888

Manufactured in the United States of America

Contents

Scott Steiner may have had humble beginnings, but he became one of the most arrogant and tasteless men in wrestling.

A Great Start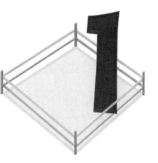

*S*cott Steiner would one day come to be known as Big Poppa Pump. By 2000, he had established himself as one of the most arrogant and tasteless men in wrestling. But this superstar of the sport had a humble beginning.

Scott Steiner was born Scott Rechsteiner on July 29, 1962, in Bay City, Michigan, little more than a year after his brother, Rick, was born on March 9, 1961. They were close in age, and they would remain close for most of their lives, ultimately following each other into wrestling.

They were both outstanding athletes in high school. They were both phenomenal wrestlers at the University of Michigan, where Scott was a two-time all-American, an award given to the best college athletes in the country. Rick made his pro wrestling debut in 1983.

Scott made his pro wrestling debut in 1986 and shortly thereafter won the World Wrestling Association (WWA) championship. He teamed with Dr. Jerry Graham to win the WWA tag team title in 1987. In 1988, he was third runner-up in the contest for *Pro Wrestling Illustrated's* Rookie of the Year. In February 1989, he teamed with Jed Grundy to win the Central Wrestling Alliance tag team belts.

The careers of both men changed remarkably in April 1989, when Scott left the CWA and joined his brother in the National Wrestling Alliance (NWA), one of the two major-league federations in North America (the other was the World Wrestling Federation, or WWF). Missy Hyatt became the brothers' manager. The brothers made an impact immediately by defeating Kevin Sullivan and Mike Rotundo at a match known as the Great American Bash on July 23, 1989, in Baltimore, Maryland.

But soon thereafter, they ran into trouble. At Fall Brawl on September 12, 1989, in Columbia, South Carolina,

> **"That girl can't be trusted."**
>
> -Scott Steiner regarding Robin Green

the Steiners battled NWA world tag team champions Jim Garvin and Michael Hayes. Nobody could tell whether Scott was tripped by Robin Green, Rick's girlfriend, or Missy Hyatt, his own manager, when he rebounded off the ropes. Hayes caught Scott in a DDT and scored the pin. Afterward, Green blamed Hyatt, and Hyatt blamed Green.

"That girl can't be trusted," Scott said of Robin in an interview. "There's evil in her eyes, and she's only going to hurt this team. I'm just looking out for Rick's best interests, but he seems to think I'm jealous."

Scott was a phenomenal wrestler at the University of Michigan and made his pro wrestling debut in 1986.

Green, who was formerly known as Fallen Angel, the evil valet of wrestler Kevin Sullivan, was not the sweet, innocent girl Rick thought she was. He suggested to several friends that he was thinking of proposing to Green. Later that week, Robin was scheduled to pick up Rick in a limousine. Rick decided that he wanted to ask her a very important question and arranged for a camera crew to record the moment.

Realizing he was running late for the meeting, Rick sent Scott to meet the limo. Scott was getting into the limo when he was beaten up by several masked thugs. One of the men kicked him in the face and midsection. Robin and the hoods sped off, leaving Scott lying on the ground.

Obviously, Robin couldn't be trusted. She changed her nickname to Woman and managed a new team of masked wrestlers called Doom. The Steiners battled Doom at Halloween Havoc on October 28, 1989, in Philadelphia. It was the first major appearance for Doom, an imposing duo whose combined weight was almost 600 pounds. Late in the match, Woman passed a foreign object to one of the masked men. The man headbutted Rick for an illegal pin and the victory.

But the Steiners would not be denied in their quest for greatness. On November 1, 1989, in Atlanta, Georgia, the Steiners stepped into the ring against NWA world tag team champions the Freebirds—

Michael Hayes and Jim Garvin. The Steiners walked out of the ring with their first world title. They beat Doom and the Freebirds in several rematches.

The Steiners finished the year on top of the wrestling world. They were the number-one team in the *Pro Wrestling Illustrated* rankings. Scott was voted

1989's Most Improved Wrestler by the readers of *PWI*. Meanwhile, the Steiners' feud with Doom intensified. On January 21, 1990, in Richmond, Virginia, the Steiners beat Doom in a match fought inside a steel cage. Then the Steiners prepared to step into the ring against their arch rivals for a key battle at Clash of the Champions X on February 6, 1990, in Corpus Christi, Texas.

By this time, Woman had dropped the contracts of Doom to go after the Four Horsemen, the wrestling clique headed by Ric Flair. A stipulation for the match was that if Doom lost, they'd have to unmask. One of the Doom members was inadvertently unmasked during the bout. He turned out to be Butch Reed. After Reed was pinned by Rick Steiner, the other member of Doom unmasked himself. It was Ron Simmons. The Steiners had humiliated their fiercest foes and had won the match!

Riding a great wave of confidence, the Steiners defeated Ole and Arn Anderson at Wrestle War '90 on February 25 in Greensboro, North Carolina. On March 11 in Atlanta, Georgia, Ole Anderson unleashed a masked duo called the Minnesota Wrecking Crew II on the Steiners. The Steiners held off the challenge when Scott pinned one of the masked men.

In April, Scott took a break from defending the world tag team title and battled NWA newcomer Bam Bam Bigelow, a 368-pound tattooed behemoth, in several matches. On April 7, in Philadelphia, Scott and Bigelow battled with remarkable ferocity. Bigelow used kicking and punching to overcome Scott's flying maneuvers, including dropkicks and suplexes. Steiner catapulted the 368-pound Bigelow into the ropes and, on the rebound, gave him a breathtaking belly-to-back suplex. Scott followed up with his Frankensteiner finisher and the pin. The next night in Atlanta, Scott beat Bigelow by disqualification.

The Minnesota Wrecking Crew II kept coming after the Steiners. On April 20 in Augusta, Georgia, the Steiners and the Wrecking Crew battled in a stretcher match, so called because the only way to win the match is by forcing your opponent to be carried away on a stretcher. After Scott pinned one member of the Crew, Rick ran outside the ring and gave the other a clothesline, knocking him onto the stretcher. Rick then wheeled the Crew member to the dressing room. But the rigorous demands of defending the world title finally caught up to the Steiners on May 19, 1990, in Washington, D.C., when they lost the tag belts to Doom. Butch Reed pinned Rick after nineteen minutes and fourteen seconds of intense, violent action.

Stunned by the loss, the Steiners couldn't regain the title in several re-matches and jumped at the chance to wrestle for the NWA's secondary tag team championship, the United States title. On

August 24, 1990, in East Rutherford, New Jersey, the Steiners won the U. S. championship from the Midnight Express. The Steiners held firm in several rematches.

While Doom feuded with the Four Horsemen—who were granted most of the world tag team title shots—the Steiners turned their attention to a couple of grungy looking rulebreakers who seemed more interested in disgusting their opponents than beating them. The team was called the Nasty Boys, and its members, Jerry Sags and Brian Knobs, did things like stuffing their opponents' heads into their sweaty armpits. Yeech! During a card in Chicago on September 30, the Nasty Boys slammed Scott through a wooden table and bloodied both Rick and Scott. The Steiners were intent on revenge.

At Halloween Havoc on October 27, 1990, Scott pinned Knobs to win the match for his team. After the match, Jerry Sags came from behind a popcorn vendor and attacked Scott while Scott was being interviewed. The teams were scheduled to meet again on November 2 in Winston-Salem, North Carolina. As the Steiners made their way to the ring, Knobs and Sags jumped Scott from behind and knocked him unconscious. Terry Taylor substituted for Scott. During a wild brawl in the ring, Scott returned to ringside and attacked the Nasty Boys. The match was declared a no-contest, in which there is no winner.

Using all of their wrestling abilities, the Steiners finally beat the Nasty Boys—on three consecutive nights!

"I don't care what the decision was, I'm gonna get my revenge on those two," Scott said. "Sags and Knobs are pretty smug right now, they think they've got the upper hand on me and Rick, but we're just getting warmed up. After we're done with the Nasty Boys, they'll be lucky to be able to chew on food, much less try another stunt like that."

The Nasty Boys attacked Scott several more times. Finally, Scott got his chance for revenge. Wrestling at full-strength, the Steiners beat the Nasty Boys on three consecutive nights. "Nobody intimidates us, especially two clowns like Knobs and Sags," Scott said. "We're definitely on our way to another world tag team title, and we won't be denied."

The Steiners were denied the world title for the rest of 1990, but the readers of *Pro Wrestling Illustrated* still voted them Tag Team of the Year. "There are a lot of great tag teams out there and I'm glad to see that the fans recognize all the hard work that we do in the ring," Scott said. "Believe me, it's not easy coming up with new moves all the time, but we make it a point to do just that, and the fans have responded in the arenas with their cheers. It really means a lot to me and Rick."

As if to show the fans their gratitude, the Steiners won the Pat O'Connor Memorial International Tag Team Championship tournament at Starrcade on December 16 in St. Louis by beating the Great Muta and Mr. Saito of Japan in the finals. It had been a great year for Scott and Rick, but the best was yet to come.

Superstars

Just about everything was going right for the Steiners. At Wrestle War '91 on February 24, Scott and Rick teamed with Sting and Brian Pillman and lost to the Four Horsemen. But two weeks later on March 9, 1991, in Montgomery, Alabama, the Steiners defeated the Freebirds—Jim Garvin and Michael Hayes—for their second National Wrestling Association (NWA) world tag team title. The brothers really didn't care that they had to give up their U. S. tag team title (wrestlers weren't allowed to hold more than one major title). They had the championship they wanted.

"This proves to the world that the Steiners are one of the greatest teams ever," Scott said. "You win one title and people can say it's a fluke. They can say to you, 'Let's see you do it again.' But when you win those belts the second time, that's something nobody can ever take away from you."

Once again, the Steiners were on top of the world. They added to their collection of championships on March 21, 1991, in Tokyo, Japan, by beating the team of Hiroshi Hase and Kensuke Sasaki for the International Wrestling Grand Prix (IWGP) tag team championship. Then they got ready for a much-anticipated event: a fan

Scott's brother and wrestling partner, Rick, has a well-deserved flamboyant

favorites versus fan favorites tag team match pitting the Steiners against Lex Luger and Sting at SuperBrawl '91 on May 19 in St. Petersburg, Florida.

It was a classic match. The wrestlers matched each other move for move, exchanging piledriver reversals, leg sweeps, suplex variations, and aerial clotheslines, in which they leaped into the air with their forearms outstretched and struck their rivals across the throat. The crowd was on their feet for most of the match. The intensity was remarkable, considering that both teams were friends and fan favorites.

But then Nikita Koloff stormed into the ring and interfered. He smacked Sting across the face with a chain. Confused, Sting fell to the canvas. Scott rolled on top of him for a pin that he really didn't want. The three-count was made, and the Steiners won the match. Afterward, all four wrestlers chased Koloff out of the ring.

After the match, Sting said, "I felt like Lex and I were taking on an army in there." Scott countered, "You haven't lived until you've experienced a Lex Luger clothesline." But the rigors of defending the world title were getting to the Steiners. In early June, Scott tore his left bicep muscle, the large muscle in the front of the upper arm.

Nevertheless, on June 12, 1991, Rick and Scott wrestled Hiroshi Hase and Masahiro Chono at Clash of the Champions XV. When Dick Slater and Dick Murdoch stormed the ring to attack the Steiners, Rick injured his left arm. Later, it was discovered that Scott's injury was serious and would sideline him for several months.

Rick teamed with several other World Championship Wrestling (WCW) wrestlers. At the Great American Bash on July 4, 1991, Rick teamed with Missy Hyatt to beat Paul E. Dangerously and Arn Anderson in a cage match. But in late July, with Scott's return still several months away, WCW officials stripped the Steiners of the world tag team title. The belts were put up for grabs in a tournament and were won by the team of Arn Anderson and Larry Zbyszko. They beat Bill Kazmaier and Rick in the championship match on September 5, 1991.

Scott returned to the ring at Halloween Havoc on October 27, 1991, in Chattanooga, Tennessee. He teamed with Rick, Sting, and seven foot, seven inch El Gigante to battle Barry Windham, Abdullah the Butcher, Big Van Vader, and Diamond Studd in a Chamber of Horrors cage match. The Steiners' team won when Abdullah was placed in an electric chair.

The Steiners lost the IWGP tag team title on November 5. Scott failed to appear for a scheduled title defense against Hase and the Great Muta. Rick was allowed to choose a partner, and he chose Scott Norton. Hase and Muta beat them for the belts.

The Steiners returned as a tag team in mid-November and racked up victories

As his career progressed, Scott gained confidence in his abilities.

in Greensboro and Charlotte, North Carolina. They defeated WCW world tag team champions the Enforcers (Arn Anderson and Larry Zbyszko) by disqualification in matches they dominated. "Yeah, I was sidelined for a couple of months, but I'm back now and I'm 100 percent," Scott said. "Just ask Arn Anderson or Larry Zbyszko if either of them thinks that I'm a pushover since I've returned. And I have some more news for Anderson and Zbyszko: Those world belts are just on loan to them. They'll be back around Rick's and my waists before they know what hit them."

The Steiners feuded with Anderson, Zbyszko, and Bobby Eaton but kept having their attempts to regain the belts turned back. The Steiners compiled a remarkable win-loss record over the following months but couldn't win the title. At SuperBrawl II on February 29, 1992, in Milwaukee, Wisconsin, Anderson and Eaton—who had won the belts on January 16, 1992—beat Rick and Scott by disqualification.

Scott pinned Eaton after delivering a Frankensteiner, but the pin was nullified because referee Randy Anderson had been knocked out by Rick's suplex. It was another frustrating setback for the Steiners. When they defeated Anderson and Eaton on March 8 in Atlanta, Georgia, it was in a nontitle match; the belts weren't on the line.

Scott not only feuded with other wrestlers but with referees, too.

"I guess we gave 'em something to think about," Scott said. "We always knew we could take 'em. Now they know." But Paul E. Dangerously, manager of the champions, discounted the victory, saying, "It was a nontitle match and I don't care what anybody says, when the belt isn't on the line, you let up. It's only natural. I'm sure the Steiners are blowing their horns about this one. Good! Let 'em have that false confidence."

The feud was intense. Eaton and Anderson were barely holding on to the title. Their title matches against the Steiners kept ending in interference from other wrestlers. The use of foreign objects and disqualifications also were common. On

March 31 in East Rutherford, New Jersey, the Steiners beat Anderson and Eaton by disqualification after Dangerously interfered.

On April 16 in Columbia, South Carolina, the Steiners battled the champions to a double-countout, in which both sides were out of the ring for twenty seconds and were disqualified by the referee. On May 3 in Chicago, the Steiners walked into the ring at the UIC (University of Illinois-Chicago) Pavillion determined to wrest the belts from their enemies. This time, they wouldn't be denied, and they beat Anderson and Eaton for their third world tag team title.

"Our waists were starting to feel naked without belts around them," Scott said. "We had to give up the belts the second time because I was injured, and I always felt kind of lousy about that, but there was never a doubt we'd win them back. It was just a question of when."

But the Steiners had a new team to worry about: Steve Williams and Terry Gordy, the powerful American brawlers who had been wrestling in Japan. When Williams and Gordy returned to America, they set their sights on the WCW world tag team title. At Beach Blast '92 on June 20 in Mobile, Alabama, the invaders battled the Steiners for thirty minutes to a draw.

The period between June 26 and July 5, 1992, was a remarkable ten days for the Steiners. On June 26, they traveled to Tokyo

Scott hangs on the ropes during a heated battle.

and won their second IWGP tag team title from Vader and Bigelow. On July 5 in Atlanta, they put their belts on the line against Williams and Gordy.

Late in the match, Scott connected with a Frankensteiner on Williams and began to celebrate instead of moving in for the pin. Gordy illegally entered the ring and nailed Scott from behind with a clothesline, knocking Scott to the mat. With Scott prone on the mat, Williams scored the pin; Rick was too late to break it up.

"We'll be back," Rick guaranteed. "You can bet on that. And when we do come back, Gordy and Williams are gonna wish they were back in Japan."

The Steiners beat Gordy and Williams, but only in nontitle matches. On July 30 in Roanoke, Virginia, Rick and Scott beat Gordy and Williams, but the champs retained the belts. On August 2 in Baltimore, Maryland, Gordy and Williams beat the brothers in a best-of-three-falls match.

Gordy pinned Scott in the third fall as Williams held Scott's leg. On September

23 in Yokohama, Japan, the brothers successfully defended the IWGP tag belts against Hiroshi Hase and Kensuke Sasaki. Rick tore his right pectoral muscle (a muscle in the chest) during the match. He would need to rest three months while the injury healed.

So Scott concentrated on singles wrestling. On September 29 in Atlanta, he stepped into the ring against WCW television champion Rick Steamboat, whom many consider one of the most talented wrestlers in the sport's history. It was an outstanding match. Neither man could gain a significant advantage.

Late in the match, Steiner reversed a painful wristlock, in which his wrist was twisted behind his back, but Steamboat elbowed him in the head. Steamboat came off the ropes with a cross-bodyblock, but Steiner got out of the way and Steamboat flew over the top rope to the arena floor. When Steamboat stepped back into the ring, Scott threw him to the mat for the pin. Scott had his first major singles title.

"Whoever thinks Scott Steiner is strictly a tag team wrestler should have been in that ring tonight," Steamboat said. "He is excellent, and there is no embarrassment in losing to him." During Rick's absence, Scott teamed with other wrestlers and doggedly defended the TV title.

Rick returned earlier than expected, and he and Scott defended the IWGP belts against Tony Halme and Scott Norton on November 22 in Tokyo. But Rick was still feeling pain in his torn pectoral muscle and was in no condition to wrestle. Norton and Halme won the match and the belts.

Maybe Rick shouldn't have returned before the injury was fully healed. But there was another reason for the loss: The Steiners had other things on their minds. In early December, the Steiners announced that they were leaving WCW to join the rival World Wrestling Federation (WWF). Wrestling's tag team landscape was about to change dramatically.

The Rigors of Wrestling

Rick and Scott Steiner made their WWF debuts on December 14, 1992, in Green Bay, Wisconsin, and they defeated Rick Warner and Scott Colton. The only remarkable thing about the match was that one of the best tag teams in the world now made its home in the WWF. And that meant trouble for WWF world tag team champions Money Inc., the team of Ted DiBiase and Irwin R. Schyster.

The Steiners made their WWF pay-per-view debut at the Royal Rumble on January 24, 1993, and they beat the Beverly Brothers. Scott used his Frankensteiner to pin Blake Beverly. The Steiners soared close to the top of the WWF tag team rankings. The brothers were in line for a match at WrestleMania IX against Money Inc. when Hulk Hogan and Brutus Beefcake returned to the WWF and targeted DiBiase and Schyster. So the Steiners wrestled the Headshrinkers instead, a match Scott won by pinning one of them after a Frankensteiner.

The Steiners were active wrestlers. During a seven-day stretch early in the year, they wrestled once a day every day in seven

Even though Rick and Scott Steiner were in excellent health, their grueling schedule was beginning to take a toll on their bodies.

different cities, winning five times with two double-countouts. "My back was killing me and Rick's knees were hurting bad," Scott told *The Wrestler* magazine. "Friends kept calling us up and congratulating us on our run, but what did we have to show for it? We were tired, hurt, and we still didn't have the WWF world tag team title. I felt like we killed ourselves for nothing."

Despite protests by WWF promoters, the Steiners reduced their schedule to five matches per week, then four. The Steiners piled up victories-by-disqualification over Money Inc. The champions got themselves disqualified, walked away from the ring, and even used Schyster's briefcase to pummel the Steiners.

At the King of the Ring pay-per-view on June 13 in Dayton, Ohio, the Steiners teamed with the Smokin' Gunns to beat Money Inc. and the Headshrinkers. A day later, the Steiners and Money Inc. battled in a tag team match in Columbus, Ohio. All four men were in the ring when Rick powerslammed Schyster and stunned him with a clothesline. Scott tagged in, rocked Schyster with a Frankensteiner, and then covered him for the pin. The Steiners were the WWF world tag team champions, and only the third team in history to win the WWF and WCW/NWA world tag team titles.

Two days later in Rockford, Illinois, the Steiners lost the title to Money Inc. But on June 19 in St. Louis, Missouri, the brothers dominated from the opening bell and won their second WWF world tag team title. The title changes on June 16 and 19, 1993, were the two fastest in WWF history.

Their schedule remained grueling, but Rick and Scott were determined to keep the belts. On June 30 in Atlantic City, New Jersey, they beat Money Inc. when Scott pinned DiBiase. They piled up victories over Money Inc. They faced a huge challenge at the Providence Civic Center on August 12 when they battled the half-ton team of Bam Bam Bigelow and Yokozuna. Rick escaped a bearhug by Bigelow but was attacked by flagpole-bearing Mr. Fuji, manager of the challengers. Fuji swung the pole, Rick ducked, and Fuji accidentally struck Bigelow. Rick rolled up Bigelow for the pin to retain the belts.

The Steiners faced another tough challenge at SummerSlam on August 30 in Auburn Hills, Michigan. Their opponents were the underrated Heavenly Bodies, the team of Jim Del Ray and Tom Prichard, managed by Jim Cornette. Cornette interfered several times, using his tennis racket on Rick and Scott, but Scott used his Frankensteiner on Del Ray and Rick scored the pin.

Their next major test came against the Quebecers on September 13 on *Monday Night Raw* at Madison Square Garden in New York. The match was contested under province of Quebec rules, meaning the title could change hands on a disqualification. Johnny Polo, manager of the Quebecers, came to the ring with a hockey stick during the match. When Polo got into the ring, Rick punched him. The stick landed inside the ring. Scott picked it up and started hitting Polo with the stick. Referee Dave Hebner only saw Scott hit one of the Quebecers with the stick and disqualified the Steiners, costing Rick and Scott the tag team championship.

The readers of *Pro Wrestling Illustrated* voted the Steiners as Tag Team of the Year for the second time in four years, but that was of little consolation to Rick and Scott. They were burnt out from the competition. Their injuries were piling up. Rick and Scott hurt so badly that they could barely sleep at night. They feared becoming cripples before they hit middle age. The Steiners faced enormous fan and media pressure in the United States.

In mid-February 1994, the Steiners decided to move to Japan. Immediately, they scored an impressive victory over Mike Enos and Bobby Eaton, then defeated Kensuke Sasaki and Jushin Luger in front of a sellout crowd at Sumo Hall in Tokyo. Luger and Sasaki were considered two of the finest Japanese wrestlers.

In Japan, the Steiners wrestled whenever they wanted to, didn't have to deal with the media (which cared mostly about the Japanese wrestlers), gave their injuries time to heal, and wrestled only against top tag teams. Finally, in February 1995, a year after he and his brother had left for Japan, Scott said, "The competition in Japan has been great. We got a break from the pressure. Maybe it's time to come back."

But the Steiners made a decision that shocked everyone, especially WWF and WCW officials. Instead of returning to the WWF or WCW, they went to Extreme Championship Wrestling (ECW), a regional federation located in the northeastern United States. "You're at the highest risk when your body is exhausted and your resistance is down," Scott said. "That's a medical fact. If you're fresh and healthy, it's going to take a lot for you to get hurt, but if

Scott flies through the air clutching a member of the Harlem Heat wrestling team.

you're tired and your body is worn down
the slightest hit can cause serious injury.
like it in ECW because we don't have to
wrestle every night or travel all over the
country week in and week out. Basically, we
wrestle in Pennsylvania and other parts o
the Northeast and Florida, but it's mostly by
cars and very short plane trips. You know
what? I feel more like a human being in this
federation than I ever have before."

On July 28, 1995, in Middletown, New
York, the Steiners beat Dudley Dudley
and Vampire Warrior. On August 5 in
Philadelphia, the Steiners teamed with
Eddy Guerrero against 2 Cold Scorpio, Dean
Malenko, and Cactus Jack in a six-person
match. The Steiners used devastating

uplexes on their opponents, but the match ended with Malenko pinning Guerrero. A few weeks later, the Steiners beat 2 Cold Scorpio and Chris Benoit.

Overall, the Steiners enjoyed their schedule. They wrestled whom they wanted, when they wanted. The urge to wrestle in major pay-per-views for major championships was occasionally tempting, but they resisted the temptation.

"Everybody's been waiting for us to make our move for the past year, but we'll have the final say in this matter," Rick said. "It's our life, and we're going to keep it that way." The Steiners were one of the most sought-after tag teams in the world. They had earned the right to do things their way.

Home Again

The fans wanted them back. The promoters wanted them back. Although there was certainly no lack of good tag teams in WCW and the WWF the void created by the Steiners' absence couldn't be filled. Even the Road Warriors Hawk and Animal, the dominant tag team of the 1980s, couldn't create enough excitement to satisfy WCW fans.

And so, in late March 1996, the Steiners, unable to further resist temptation, and realizing that the time was right, returned to WCW. It was not long before they regained their standing as one of the best tag teams ever. One of their first orders of business was to challenge the Road Warriors in a feud that matched the best team of the 1980s against the best team of the 1990s. Both teams were packed with power and skill, and the fans were thrilled to watch their closely fought battles.

There was no clear winner in these matches, which

"This is a great achievement for us."

-Scott Steiner on winning the fourth title

turned out to be ultimate tests of skill and perseverance for both teams. The great teams exchanged victories. After their battles with the Warriors, the brothers piled up victories against other WCW teams. They humbled Scott Norton and Ice Train at the Great American Bash on June 16, 1996, in Baltimore, Maryland, and beat world tag team champions Harlem Heat (the team of Booker T and Stevie Ray) by disqualification on June 30 in New York City. But Harlem Heat couldn't get away with the belts on July 24, 1996, in Cincinnati, Ohio, where the Steiners beat them for their fourth WCW world tag team title (and first since 1992).

"This is a great achievement for us," Scott said. "A lot of people were ruling us out when we were away in Japan, but we proved that we can come back better than ever. This justifies our plans all along. We knew we needed to take time off to regroup and get our bodies back in top wrestling shape, and now we're seeing the payoff."

But the payoff was temporary: Three days later in Dayton, Ohio, Harlem Heat regained the title from Scott and Rick. At Clash of the Champions XXXIII on August 15 in Denver, Colorado, the referee stopped a three-way match involving the Steiners, Harlem Heat, and the team of Lex Luger and Sting when he saw Scott Hall and Kevin Nash attack Luger and Sting at ringside.

Scott tangles with world tag team champions Harlem Heat (Booker T and Stevie Ray).

Hall and Nash were members of the newly formed New World Order (NWO), a rulebreaking clique designed to overtake WCW. The Steiners did their best to stay clear of the WCW versus NWO war, which had engulfed the federation. They had only one thing on their minds: regaining the world tag team title.

Unfortunately, Scott wasn't wrestling in peak physical condition. He was suffering from severe back pain and had trouble executing even the simplest maneuvers. In September, Scott decided to take time off. For the rest of 1996 and into early 1997, Rick wrestled on his own.

Scott returned to action on January 22, 1997, at Clash of the Champions XXXIV.

n Milwaukee. Scott and Rick beat the Amazing French-Canadiens, Luc and Pierre Oulette. Three days later, they faced WCW world tag team champions Nash and Hall at Souled Out in Cedar Rapids, Iowa. The NWO wrestlers had their own referee for the match, Nick Patrick, but he was knocked out during a scuffle and replaced by WCW referee Randy Anderson. When Scott pinned Hall, Anderson made the three-count.

The Steiners appeared to be the new world tag team champions, but the decision was reversed by WCW senior vice president—and NWO flunky—Eric Bischoff because the wrong referee had made the count. Nash and Hall were still champions. The Steiners could no longer avoid the WCW versus NWO war. The were stuck in the middle.

On April 6, the Steiners were scheduled to battle Nash and Hall at the Coliseum in Tupelo, Mississippi. Hall however, couldn't wrestle because o personal reasons. When WCW ruled tha Nash would have to defend the title on hi own, Nash refused unless WCW agreed t allow Nick Patrick to serve as referee. Wher a WCW official went to Nash's dressing room to talk with Nash, he was barred from entering by Syxx, a member of the New World Order.

Then, the Steiners approached Nash' locker room door. Nash opened the door spit in Scott's face, and jumped back inside

WCW's security force were trying to restrain Scott when he swung his arm and struck a police officer. Scott was arrested, handcuffed, and escorted from the building. The charges were eventually dropped, but the rivalry between the Steiners and the NWO was hotter than ever.

At Uncensored on May 18 in Charleston, South Carolina, Team NWO (consisting of Hall, Nash, Hulk Hogan, and Randy Savage) beat Team WCW (the Steiners, the Giant, and Lex Luger) and Team Piper (a foursome of wrestlers loyal to veteran grappler Roddy Piper). The Steiners scored more victories over Harlem Heat, but they were frustrated. They wanted to take on Hall and Nash.

The Steiners got a shot against Nash and Hall at Road Wild on August 9 in Sturgis, North Dakota, but their victory by disqualification didn't earn them the world tag team championship. Then, on September 19, 1997, Nash suffered torn ligaments in his right knee while wrestling in Seattle, Washington. The fate of the WCW world tag team title was in the air: How would WCW officials rule on this issue? Would they wait for Nash to return? Would they strip Nash and Hall of the belts?

WCW officials ruled that Hall could choose a new partner for his title defenses. On October 13, 1997, on *Nitro* in Tampa, Florida, Rick and Scott took on Hall and

Scott gets an earful from an unidentified opponent.

Syxx. The makeshift tag team was no match for the Steiners, who won their fifth WCW world title that night.

They were active champions, beating Public Enemy in a type of match called a Philadelphia streetfight on *Nitro* on November 3, holding off the challenge of Harlem Heat, and beating Dave Taylor and Steven Regal at World War III on

November 23 in Auburn Hills, Michigan. They even found time for some singles wrestling, but Scott told *The Wrestler* magazine: "I'm a tag team wrestler, and I'm happy doing it. I take the singles matches here and there, but I believe my brother and I are the greatest tag team ever. A lot of people I talk to tell me that, too. We want to keep building on that reputation we have for as long as possible." Their reputation was solid, or so it seemed.

Clash of the Steiners

It didn't seem possible that anything could tear apart the Steiner brothers. They had always stood by each other through injuries, setbacks, and personal problems. Rick and Scott had the kind of bond that only a tag team of brothers could have. They had a blood bond.

But on *Nitro* on January 6, 1998, the bond between the brothers seemed to be breaking. Scott arrived late for a scheduled tag team title defense against Scott Norton and Vincent. Rick was forced to wrestle on his own, and, although Rick won, he was beaten up by his opponent after the match. Scott, dressed in street clothes, finally showed up and saved him.

Two nights later at Thunder, Scott never tried to tag his brother in a match against Konnan and Buff Bagwell. The Steiners won, but Rick never got into the ring because Scott refused to tag him. "I've never seen two tag team partners communicate and work as well as these two men, until now," said Ted DiBiase, manager of the Steiners. "Now it's like whenever I'm supposed to be in the gym with Rick while he's working out, I have Scott asking me why I'm not doing this or that with him and vice

Scott gets caught between Konnan and Buff Bagwell.

versa. I hate to say it, but this is about to explode. I've tried to get them to sit down and talk out whatever this problem they have is, but it doesn't work. I don't know what to do. They don't even like traveling together anymore."

Scott contended: "We're winning. That's all that matters. I'm still committed to the team, and I plan to stay committed. I get delayed for one of our matches and I try to give him a break in the other and he's mad? That sounds ridiculous to me. I think he owes me an apology for overreacting."

The tension between the brothers rose on January 12 in Jacksonville, Florida, when Hall and Nash beat them for the WCW world tag team title. Rumors circulated that Scott had been secretly meeting with the New World Order and was considering signing with the group. The Steiners regained the belts from Nash and Hall on February 9 in El Paso, Texas, and they prepared for a rematch at SuperBrawl VIII on February 22 in San Francisco.

Nobody could have imagined what happened that night: During the match, Scott attacked Rick, enabling Nash and Hall to win the match and the world championship. Twenty-four hours later on *Nitro*, Scott emerged with a new head of bleached-blond hair and a bad attitude. He was suddenly friends with former rival and fellow NWO wrestler Buff Bagwell. For the first time in their lives, he and Rick were on

Scott tussles with a member of the **NWO**.

opposite sides. Scott was a member of the hated NWO and Rick was their target!

At Spring Stampede on April 19 in Denver, Rick and Lex Luger beat Scott and Bagwell. It was almost painful to watch the brothers on opposite sides. On April 22 in Columbia, South Carolina, Scott interfered during a match pitting Rick and Luger against Scott Norton and Bagwell.

Late in the match, Scott hit his brother with a chair and rolled Bagwell on top of him for the pin. The brothers briefly reunited but split again. An injury suffered by Rick kept him and Scott from wrestling one-on-one until Fall Brawl on September 13, 1998, when they battled to a no-decision.

A rematch was scheduled for Halloween Havoc on October 25 in Las Vegas. The brothers were supposed to meet in a singles match, but things changed when Buff Bagwell told Rick he wanted to be in his corner. Scott then challenged Bagwell and Rick to face him and the Giant, with the WCW world tag team belts on the line. The belts were actually held by Hall and the Giant, but Scott was allowed to defend them on Hall's behalf. WCW executive committee chairman J. J. Dillon also stipulated that if Scott and the Giant lost the belts, Scott would have to face Rick in a fifteen-minute singles match.

When the bell rang, Rick stunned his brother with punches, clotheslines, and suplexes. He went in for the pin but was stopped by Bagwell, who wanted to make the pin himself. But instead of covering Scott, Bagwell kicked Rick in the groin and ran out of the ring. Scott held Rick as the Giant tried a dropkick from the top rope. Rick moved out of the way, and the Giant struck Scott. Rick then covered the Giant for the pin and the world tag team title.

Then Scott battled Rick in a fifteen-minute match. Rick dominated until Bagwell, dressed as then-president Bill Clinton, interfered and laid him out. But Scott missed with a clothesline, and Rick scored the pin to finish off what turned out to be a great night for one Steiner brother and a horrible night for the other.

Although he often brawled with opponents and officials, Scott remained a fan favorite.

Over the following weeks, Scott went on a rampage, attacking officials and wrestlers. The change in his attitude was shocking. He was cocky and belligerent, and he loved showing off his biceps. He was now known as Big Poppa Pump. He had gone from being one of the hardest working, most unassuming wrestlers in the world to being one of the most flamboyant.

At World War III on November 22 in Auburn Hills, Michigan, Rick and Scott battled to a no-decision (in a no-decision, the match never reaches a conclusion or a time limit). Scott and Buff both attacked Rick before Bill Goldberg saved the day and left Scott lying on the mat. But Scott would not be denied, and on December 28 in Baltimore, Maryland, he finished the year on a high note by beating Konnan for the WCW TV title.

Suddenly, Scott was regarded as one of the top singles wrestlers in the world. He ranked as high as number two in *Pro Wrestling Illustrated*'s Top Ten. He did everything to anger the fan favorites. He knew that the best way to get Diamond

Dallas Page's (DDP) attention was to insult Kimberly, Page's wife, so he did.

The result was a hot feud between DDP and Big Poppa Pump. They wrestled at SuperBrawl '99 on February 21 in Oakland, California. There was also a stipulation: If Steiner won, Kimberly would have to stay by his side for thirty days. Page seemed on his way to victory when Bagwell interfered. Steiner placed Page in his Steiner recliner finishing hold, and DDP passed out in pain. Steiner had Kimberly.

Page wanted revenge, but the fans perceived him as a whining brat when he complained about Bagwell's interference. Suddenly, and for no apparent reason, the fans had switched sides in the Steiner

WCW officials banned Scott's television appearances for his insulting remarks directed at Ric Flair, the WWF, and WCW.

versus Page feud. Page was the bad guy. Steiner had become the fan favorite. He was an unlikely fan favorite. In fact, WCW officials reprimanded Scott for several sexually suggestive remarks he made on *Nitro*.

Scott soon lost the belt to Booker T at Uncensored on March 14 in Louisville, Kentucky, when Bagwell's interference backfired. But that was the least of Scott's problems. Nearly a year earlier, Scott had been arrested and charged with striking a Georgia Department of Transportation worker with his pickup truck. The man was not seriously injured, but Scott was sentenced to ten days in jail after pleading guilty to charges of aggravated assault and making terroristic threats. "I just apologize that this happened," Scott said.

Scott also lost several one-on-one matches against Rick but cemented his reputation as an outcast when he beat Booker T in the finals of a tournament for the U.S. title on April 11 in Tacoma, Washington. Scott struck Booker T in the face with a foreign object, then proclaimed, "Ain't nothing like winning a title in front of a bunch of stupid rednecks." Scott's remarks nearly resulted in a physical confrontation between him and several fans.

Normalcy was restored, at least briefly, on May 9 in St. Louis, when Scott tripped Booker T and helped his brother win the WCW TV title. One match later, Rick hit Bagwell with a chair, enabling Scott to retain the U.S. title. Both Steiners attacked Bill Goldberg and Sting at the conclusion of their bout.

By this time, the friendship between Scott and Buff Bagwell had disintegrated. "The only thing finer than Scotty Steiner is the Steiner brothers working together," Scott boasted. But there was nothing fine about the Steiners, who sicced dogs on Sting at the Great American Bash on June 13, 1999, in Baltimore.

Scott beat Chris Benoit for the TV title on October 24, 1999, in Las Vegas, but he was too injured to defend the belt at Mayhem on November 21. Scott Hall was awarded the title. On January 3, 2000,

Scott and Nash lost to David Flair and Crowbar in the finals of a tournament for the vacant WCW world tag team title. And in February 2000, WCW officials banned Scott's television appearances for his inflammatory remarks directed at Ric Flair, the WWF, and WCW. Big Poppa Pump was out of control.

Singles
Superstar

Big Poppa Pump returned to *Nitro* on March 20, 2000, in Gainesville, Florida, and he teamed with Jeff Jarrett against Sid Vicious and Hulk Hogan. Steiner was outstanding. A week later in South Padre Island, Texas, Jarrett and Scott defeated Curt Hennig and Bagwell.

WCW underwent a dramatic change on April 10, 2000, in Denver. That night's edition of *Nitro* ushered in a new era for WCW, in which the young guns would get preference over the older stars for title matches and main events. Eric Bischoff, WCW senior vice president, and head writer Vince Russo stripped all WCW champions of their titles. Many figured that Big Poppa Pump would be one of the older stars who would suffer from this reorganization. Steiner made it clear that that wouldn't happen.

One edition of *Nitro* seemed to be the Big Poppa Pump show. He made no fewer than six appearances, doing such things as calling out (challenging a person to come out and fight) Vince Russo, challenging Booker T, getting attacked by

Tank Abbott, and going head-to-head with his brother. "That's because nobody gave me the chance to speak my mind," Scott said. "I had to make my own opportunities, because nobody was handing me a damn thing. What you're seeing now is purely the creation of Scott Steiner. Nothing was ever given to me."

Scott certainly earned the WCW U.S. title he won at Spring Stampede on April 17 in Chicago, Illinois. He beat Mike Awesome in the semifinals of the tournament, then beat Sting in the finals. Scott renewed an old rivalry on April 18 in Rockford, Illinois. He appeared to be on the verge of beating WCW world champion Jeff Jarrett when Booker T charged

Scott gets thrown headfirst to the mat by a formidable opponent.

he ring and kicked Scott in the back. arrett was disqualified but retained the vorld title. Big Poppa Pump and Booker T rawled the following week on *Nitro*.)n *Nitro* on May 29 in Salt Lake City, Jtah, Big Poppa Pump laid a bruising on hane Douglas. Scott and Nash wreaked navoc on WCW and targeted Vince Russo or pain.

Bash at the Beach on July 9, 2000, in)aytona Beach, Florida, was an eventful night for Big Poppa Pump. First, he was disqualified from his U.S. title defense against Mike Awesome for using the teiner recliner, a move WCW commis- ioner Ernest Miller had banned. Miller ook the additional step of stripping

Steiner of the title. Then Scott attacked Nash during his match against Bill Goldberg. Goldberg speared and jack-hammered Nash to win the match, and afterward, Scott attacked Nash again.

Big Poppa Pump was amazingly ruthless. He was always angry. The other wrestlers in WCW granted him a wide berth in the locker room. He faced off against the National Football League's Jumbo Elliot in a jawing match. He even beat up WCW commissioner Ernest Miller. Although the buffed-up Big Poppa Pump was relying on a ground-based attack, instead of on the aerial and suplex attack of his tag team days, he was more effective than ever.

"Happiness is like poison," Scott told *The Wrestler.* "One taste and you're dead. If you're happy, you're satisfied. And if you're satisfied, you become complacent. And if you're a complacent wrestler, I come along and kick your [butt]."

Even Goldberg, one of the most feared men in wrestling, wasn't safe from Scott's crazy behavior. One night, Big Poppa Pump kidnapped Goldberg's girlfriend. At Fall Brawl on September 17 in Buffalo, New York, Scott beat Goldberg in a no-disqualification match by using a steel chair and a lead pipe to render Goldberg unconscious.

He couldn't be stopped. He wouldn't be stopped. On November 26, in

Milwaukee, Wisconsin, Big Poppa Pump prepared for one of the most important matches of his life: a main event steel cage/strait jacket showdown against WCW world champion Booker T at the Mayhem pay-per-view. Scott gained the early advantage with a clothesline and a belly-to-back suplex. Then he clotheslined Booker T and flexed his biceps to the fans. He dropped Booker T to the mat, then covered him for a two-count.

Scott grabbed the straight jacket but couldn't get it on Booker T. Booker T gained control of the straight jacket and placed it on Big Poppa Pump. Then he grabbed a chair and hit Steiner twice over the head. Scott ripped his arms out of the strait jacket and took it off. He used his Steiner recliner on Booker T, who managed to escape.

Scott climbed to the top rope and leaped toward Booker T, who caught him in the midsection. Booker T then clotheslined Scott and floored him with a swinging neckbreaker. The challenger was in trouble. Big Poppa Pump grabbed a chair and smashed Booker T over the head. Then he clamped on the Steiner recliner. Booker T finally submitted, and Scott won his first WCW world heavyweight championship.

And yet, he didn't seem to care. "So win the title. So what?" Scott said. "What's so special about that? I'm

Scott flies toward the mat, bringing his opponent with him.

already the greatest wrestler in the world. I should be the champion. And I would be, but WCW finds a new way to screw me out of the title every week. They've been doing it for years. Everybody knows I'm the baddest man in the world and the belt should be around my waist, but that won't happen because I'm too controversial. So week after week, I get a knife in my back. And people wonder why I'm so nasty. You have any idea how that makes me feel?"

Nobody knows why Scott became so angry, but it's a shame he couldn't enjoy his long-awaited championship. Scott was just as bitter on March 25, 2001, when he lost the world title to Booker T.

Scott may have been the bad boy of professional wrestling, but he becar
one of the best wrestlers ever.

But with an amazing record that includes world tag team championships in the WWF, WCW, and Japan, and major singles championships in WCW, Scott has established himself as one of the greatest wrestlers ever. That's something not even he can deny.

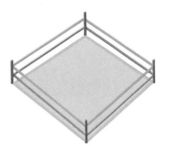

Glossary

belly-to-back suplex Offensive maneuver in which the attacker lifts his opponent upside-down, then falls backward so that the opponent lands on his back.

clothesline Offensive maneuver in which the attacker sticks out his arm and jams it against his opponent's neck, usually knocking the air out of his victim.

countout Wrestlers are required to be in the ring at all times. Whenever a wrestler

leaves the ring, the referee starts a count.
When he or she reaches twenty, the
wrestler is counted out and loses the
match by disqualification.

DDT Offensive maneuver in which the
attacker grabs his opponent in a facelock,
wraps one arm around the opponent's neck,
then drops to the mat, sending his victim's
head into the canvas.

disqualification Ruling by the referee in
which a wrestler automatically loses a
match for violating a rule.

draw In wrestling, a match in which neither
wrestler wins; a tie.

feud A series of matches between two wrestlers or two tag teams. Many times, one wrestler will bad-mouth the other wrestler or will sneak attack the wrestler.

foreign object Illegal object used in the ring, such as a chair or a pencil.

Frankensteiner Scott Steiner's favorite finishing maneuver. Scott sends his opponent into the ropes, then leaps into the air with his legs extended in front of him and in the direction of his opponent. Scott wraps his legs around his opponent's head and scissors them together, then arches backward and swings underneath his opponent, forcing the opponent to leave his feet as his head is driven into the mat.

jackhammer To lift an opponent up and drive him into the ground.

main event Featured match at a wrestling show, usually the last match of the night.

pin When either both shoulders or both shoulder blades are held in contact with the mat for three continuous seconds. A pin ends a match.

powerslam Offensive maneuver in which the attacker catches his opponent rebounding off the ropes, lifts him in the air, and slams him to the mat.

rulebreaker In wrestling, a bad guy, generally someone disliked by the fans; so called because he violates the rulebook.

swinging neckbreaker Offensive move in which the attacker grabs his opponent by the neck and snaps him to the mat.

tag team A team of two or more wrestlers. Only one wrestler is allowed in the ring at a time.

For More Information

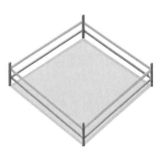

Magazines

Pro Wrestling Illustrated, The Wrestler, Inside Wrestling, Wrestle America, and *Wrestling Superstars*
London Publishing Co.
7002 West Butler Pike
Ambler, PA 19002

WOW Magazine
McMillen Communications
P.O. Box 500

Missouri City, TX 77459-9904
Fax: (281) 261-5999
e-mail: woworder@mcmillencomm.com

Web Sites

Professional Wrestling Online Museum
http://www.wrestlingmuseum.com

Pro Wrestling Torch
http://www.pwtorch.com

World Championship Wrestling
http://www.wcw.com

World Wrestling Federation
http://www.wwf.com

For Further Reading

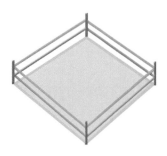

Albano, Lou, Bert Randolph Sugar, and
Michael Benson. *The Complete
Idiot's Guide to Pro Wrestling*.
2nd ed. New York: Alpha Books, 2000.

Archer, Jeff. *Theater in a Squared
Circle*. New York: White-Boucke
Publishing, 1998.

Cohen, Dan. *Wrestling Renegades:
An In-Depth Look at Today's*

Superstars of Pro Wrestling.
New York: Archway, 1999.

Conner, Floyd. *Wrestling's Most
Wanted: The Top 10 Book
of Pro Wrestling's Outrageous
Performers, Punishing Piledrivers,
and Other Oddities.* Washington,
DC: Brassey's Inc., 2001.

Hofstede, David. *Slammin': Wrestling's
Greatest Heroes and Villains.*
New York: ECW Press, 1999.

Mazer, Sharon. *Professional Wrestling:
Sport and Spectacle.* Jackson, MS:
University Press of Mississippi, 1998.

Myers, Robert, and Adolph Caso. *The Professional Wrestling Trivia Book.* Boston, MA: Branden Books, 1999.

Works Cited

Bagwell, Buff. "Why the World Must Fear Scott Steiner." *Pro Wrestling Illustrated,* October 1999, pp. 24–27.

Kennedy, Kostya. "Are the Steiners Getting Too Cocky for Their Own Good?" *Inside Wrestling,* August 1991, pp. 34–37.

Krewda, Frank. "Scott Steiner: Happiness Is an Unreachable Goal." *The Wrestler,* March 2001, pp. 40–43.

Mankiewicz, Brandi. "Revealed! The Fear
That Keeps the Steiners Out of WWF
and WCW!" *The Wrestler*, Winter
1995, pp. 30–33.

Rosenbaum, Dave. "Have the Steiners
Finally Caught Up to the Road
Warriors?" *The Wrestler*,
April 1998, pp. 42–45.

Rosenbaum, Dave. "Scott Steiner:
The Superstar the WWF Let Slip
Away!" *Pro Wrestling Illustrated*,
October 2000.

Index

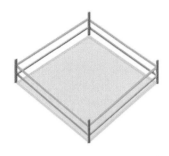

Photo Credits

All photos by Colin Bowman.

Series Design and Layout

Geri Giordano